Age Of Miracles.

Book design and cover concept by Andrea K. Boyle
Cover photo by Scott F. Lanes
Cover image manipulation by Ted Kern
Author photo taken by Scott F. Lanes
and edited by Ted Kern
Published by Fevvers Press/Andrea K. Boyle
ISBN: 978-0-6151-7031-2

Some items have been previously published in various forms in print and online media.
"Reason To Sleep Late" appeared in *Thieves Jargon* (www.thievesjargon.com), issue April 14, 2006.
"Book Cut" appeared in *Chiaroscuro* (www.chizine.com), issue #33, July-September 2007.

First Edition, October 2007.

Fevvers Press

Age of Miracles

Annie Boyle

Dedicated to the countless stellar
science fiction authors I have read,
including but certainly not limited to:

Lois McMaster Bujold, C.J. Cherryh,
Philip K. Dick, Warren Ellis,
William Gibson,
Frank Herbert, Kim Stanley Robinson,
Dan Simmons,
Neal Stephenson, Brian K. Vaughan,
and Joan D. Vinge.

CONTENTS

CONTENTS

PART I

AGE OF MIRACLES

Muse/Manifesto

i

technology is a vehicle for our humanity, it is the face of humanity, its functions reveal our designs, desires, deficiencies, deifications, discontents

either there is no future or there is no present – every second is the next one

the lover's cling of the past, we punch our way into the next age still smelling of her perfume

hurtling towards the stars, getting soul-lag

we are making our own miracles
playing god
gods are always playing

we are also not recognizing miracles when we find them

we make our own miracles, we have our own faith
fragile but focused, the power of a laser, simply light
which cuts through steel

we are also not naming them miracles when they claw on our windowpanes, covered in muck, appearing monstrosities

rough around the edges, bitter going down, miracles all the same

these are all we've got for miracles, this handful of
microprocessors, this fistful of wires, these warehouses
of metal and plastic constructs bigger than our
imaginings and smaller than our dreams

we've got these miracles, don't cry, these are all we
have, don't cry, we have all these, don't cry

ii

i take it back, there is a discrete present

a curious nook, a breath, a cradling of time

in the curve of your partner's leg, in the thrum of a
song through your body

when we say these words: I'm sorry; hold this; take
cover; will you

it is in these syllables: warmth, fall, bliss, balance,
known

it is about certainty, it is about precision

the present is in an explosion, a dive
a splash
a burn
REM sleep – sorting through the subconscious to file
our memories, images at not-quite
random to keep us sound of mind, to keep us
wondering

iii

the future blooms from dissent, inchoate arguments,
budding notations

the vanguard ever hard upon us
we strive to reach beyond the frontlines,
tear into the core

we want to manhandle, smith, mash, mould, punch it
into shapes
recognizable and original

shapes of data cards, violets, long incisors, camoflague
sports jerseys, mining picks, incandescent apples
which glow from the warmth of the cup of your hand

inventions distractions mistakes remissions, quests
prize-fights

iv

floating, falling, dancing, resting
in the dark spaces
between the stars there is reflected light

thinner than we realize, the veil of firewall
construct exquisite masks, precision languages, vast
swamps of code

the muse has never been without natural beauty
humanity has never been without muse
the beautiful nymph may have lab-grown emerald
cybernetic eyes
she may urge the body's twist away from sunlight
to the etiolated glow of a screen and guide fingertips to
plastic keys
but she was birthed shock naked
from the gnarled whorl of willow roots
on the dusky riverbank

the slender thread of green
weaves through every work
produced by our human hands

Age of Miracles 1: I Want Him Just So

Customer ID:90292051KE

clone request, tailored memory implants:

I would like to have Rudyard Kipling as a pet
no not from a babe to mould
not that challenge for this one or for me
I want him adult, grown, fully-formed, in the prime
of life – maybe thirty
don't sniff, he was a man of many travels and
accomplishments
by then, he worked fast
don't want to wait too long, you know,
or he won't make a good pet

besides, his hairline was already receding then

before WWI, before the Nobel Prize,
before "If—", before his daughter died

Yes, I'll take that one
named after a lake in the English countryside
a quaint, rural name to call out: "Rudyard!"
Sounds foreign. My exotic pet.

I will keep Rudyard Kipling in good health
brush the remaining thick black hair
take him to a groomer for the archaic moustache
get his round spectacles made out of whatever
break-resistant material is best these days
I'll supply him with toys, pen and paper,
a window bench to sit on
and when he writes a poem, I'll give him a treat
from a plastic jar

As per the contract, I will not take him
to Westminster Abbey
to Poet's Corner, to his grave
yes, yes, this psychological torture taboo

I'll put him on a choke-chain
when I take him out for walks
to the pub, to the park, to the lake
can't have him being impudent in public
I'll use chains at home, too, for training
they will encourage more satire
and more outrageous lies
great stories
which he will read aloud at parties
while I hold his leash

Age of Miracles 2: Silken Sad

Customer ID:10212051KE

Edgar Allen Poe – I will have that one, please

dying in a gutter
his eyes large, gleaming from out their shadows
swimmingly black, glistening unhealthily
like those of a ghostly Russian countess

haunted, my pet,
he will howl in the night
he will blanchen at the sight
of a commonplace bloody smear

give him something to quiet the cough, though
that just gets too disgusting
especially for dinner parties
he will crouch at my feet

but he will always be dying
dying in the gutter

FollowUp Report:
Return Requested,
Incompatible.

He is too fragile, I cannot touch him.
He is too strong, too far away
in those glistening eyes.
He understands none
of my mundane discipline.
He will not call me cousin in bed.
He is too fragile, I cannot bear
to strike him.

Age of Miracles 3: Stop Here

Customer ID:18542051LS

I have a tiny spare room on the top floor
too small for a proper guestroom, one of those rooms
that contains an extra ironing board of unknown
provenance
an architectural hiccup of a room
I'd like an Emily Dickinson to put in it
get some nice use out of the space.

There's a window, old curtains with lace,
room for a cot and a narrow dresser.
She can look out at the slice of lawn and fantasize
about Walt Whitman
(no, I don't have room for a Whitman at the moment,
though the half-off with a Dickinson does sound
like a good deal,
I don't have the room for his booming
and his blooming.
I hear he's a bitch to clean up after, mud
and grass everywhere,
and no matter what the conditioning program, he won't
keep his hands
off the maids and the gardeners.)

Just a little Emily, please,
for my useless little box room
I have an old laptop she can use

thank you for the stats, I figured she didn't eat much –

the window is screened, flies kept out
she may hear their buzzing at a distance

Age of Miracles 4: Twilight of the Gods

Customer ID:14442051EH

it's been done, I read it somewhere
a Keats persona android
but hell, Keats is beauty and beauty truth
and the truth is I want that little beauty.

A few might accuse me of an unoriginal thought
well, Keats was mocked mercilessly in his own time
and I won't have to worry about a killing article.

Oh, yes, consumption to deal with again.

I know, if I keep ordering these poets, I must expect it.
Do you have an accompanying Severn model?
The Joe can mop up when he's going
through that phase.
No? Well, do the necessary and bill the necessary.
Severn can sketch quietly
and paint a miniature of us together – Keats
and his new mistress
Preserved, tiny, precise as a microchip.

Oh, there's a deal with him and a Byron?
Yes, I'll just bet there is.
Alright, I have the space, the lawn, the follies,
the canal –
throw in the Lord.

Fanny, though –
something will have to be done about that.
Just change her name in his netting –
something more modern
less of a double-take if he moans it hopelessly,
helplessly.

He can finish his epic about the dying of the gods
about the new world order
Then if it doesn't match up to the current state of
affairs
he can be off and running on another
mythological mashup metaphor miles
and miles of verse
Enough to wrap around his heart and back.

My little beauty, a pearl of science
I must own this piece of truth.

Age of Miracles 5: Taught By Time

Customer ID: 07242052
References: Transcript #01

A breakthrough announced
They now have blind Homer

There is much controversy over his persona
It is widely suspected that the company has written him from scratch
never found an original

Who will lay claim to him now?
I propose we do, buy him for the university,
have him lecture, get him some grad student assistants

Yes, as I said, there are serious questions of credibility
but we can see how he works out
we can see how thorough the programming is
– who better to judge than the experts here?
We can see who registers for his workshops
they will come from all over, wanting to test his memory
We can see what traditions he keeps
We can keep the receipt

The price, oh, so many figures,
like ants clustered on a beach,
We will determine if the cost of keeping him
is worth the fame and recognition
and income he will bring
Homer as hostage again, perhaps –
forgive me my little joke

Approval, thank you, I will begin the process
a bit epic, if you ask me –
all these vettings and inspections
This is an unprecedented move, my colleagues,
but one that will link us with the ancients
or at least cement the ties we have been weaving
and our careers
And yes, I think in a few years, the benefits
will be over and above the initial payment
That new stadium will be built in no time

Age of Miracles 6: Among Mankind

Customer ID: 22052052JQ

pure love
I would revive that
I'm an old academic
and an even older romantic
Petrarch would be a wonderful companion
a concentration of brightness
for my darkening age

a retired academic
a retired romantic
or as retired from both of those as one can get
after having been them both for so long a life

I will take him to the market, quaint in this small town
I will take him to church, all of the three here
He will have all the unrequited loves he can desire

I want to talk with him late into the night,
speak with him about all these books on my shelves,
all my papers
Take long rambles with him through the preserve
hiking mostly in silence,
thinking on nature and God and time
concentrating on the trail, saving our breath for effort
Then, like a subject of his, we will leave the wood
and make our way among mankind
to sit in a pub, two old men, two old minds
nostalgic and self-aware and also simply
enjoying the beer and the view of the mountains

I'm sure he will enjoy this
I've read his letters and poems backwards
        and inside out,
written two dissertations on aspects of humanism
He will like this place, I assure you,
the outskirts of a university town
I can send you pictures, or you can send your
        inspectors
whatever you folks need to do
I've never done anything like this before
but I am alone, and Petrarch speaks to me

A friend in peace, a dream of the past, a real hand
        to clasp
A face to see in this ancient-timbered house other than
        my reflection
A miracle to spark my spirit, a mind
        to stimulate my own
pure love, in this scientific feat
I am alone, and Petrarch speaks to me

Age of Miracles 7:
Infinite Riches

Customer ID: 02292052SF

Christopher Marlowe
underrated, overblown
violently close to us in these times
so unknowable after all the research

Give me the reckoning for this man
I burn to know it

all my questions answered
about the Elizabethan secret service
and how one accidentally
gets a sword through the eye
He will be my direct line to knowledge
of good and evil
of Walsingham and Frizer and Raleigh
He will be my go-between, my Mephostophiles
relating to me strange tales of spies and royalty
of bets and costs and lusts and vice
He will see all this around him again
And he will put to paper the pen I will trade him

Give me the reckoning
just name your price
for Kit Marlowe, springing forth to me fully formed
sinful mouth, clever eyes, I am certain of these traits
though for the first time we will see
what he really looks like
Not the smooth face of questionable
16th century portraiture

I want this to be a one-off, I will pay for the rights
Marlowe will be mine alone

I know all this will be pricey

I can pay
I will pay
like Faustus
I will pay and pay
and pay

PART II

BETWEEN THE STARS

Winterkill

Winterkill
will be very bad this year
revealing the cold at the heart of the universe

hardly any will survive the sudden ice
the atmosphere crashing
a few organisms
tailored for the hardest and tiniest of niches

we will lose nearly everything
for a long time, an age, an age of ice
Winterkill
will bring starkly home an alien landscape
and when the thaw finally comes
the beaten and changed terrain
will be just as alien
we will have to look very closely to find the niches
we will pick our way agonizingly slowly
searching with eyes stinging, red, freezing
provided we ourselves survive the overturn
the smothering
the inevitable Winterkill

Young Law

"Come along, ma'am –
You know the law."
– a bland voice says.
Head bowed,
I whisper, "Yes."

I know the law.
I probably voted for it,
probably helped write it
back when I was so,
so much younger.
It just has to be older than that, though
it's been going on for so long.

He of the bland voice is holding my right arm.
Two others in the same military-style uniforms
make it three against one –
(I am wearing plain loose outfit of faded black
– no, dark blue)
the two following behind, they sneer a little
they mutter to each other
about trivial things, sports scores,
they look at me a little
they likely fear,
just a little.
But they are so brash, so young.

An abrupt turn, a sliding door,
and we are in the room,
myself and he of the bland voice.
The two hover at the doorway.
It is the room,
it is a small room
the walls are white
– no, lightly grey.
The chair is in the middle.
It looks like a dentist's examination chair.

A weak voice inside me protests:
But I am young, I am still young!
This is not the right age,
we set it too low. I am young!
I say nothing. It is not true.
I am here, my time has come,
I am old.

Two, three steps and with firmness
I am sat on the chair.
The cushions shine like vinyl but they are
not slippery. My legs swing into line.
My arms on the armrests,
my hands gripping involuntarily
at the curved ends.
I am sitting in it now, the black chair
– no, very, very dark grey.
Like sitting, leaning slightly, in a dentist's chair.
Except for the headpiece
the gear on the shiny swivel arm
attached near the top.

The piece is swung around,
it curves slightly over my head.
The ear part is slid onto my left ear
fitted snugly.
The whole thing is locked into place.
I realize that there are now metal bands on the armrest
and stout clasps around my shins.
There is no where to go
out of this small room.
They just don't want anything to go wrong.
I don't want anything to go wrong either.
Nightmare situation,
some poor person having something slip
and the pellet going in wrong, just lodging
in the flesh,
and being lifted by the guards
back into place
and having to do it all over.

I am locked in.
The guards disappear.
I am alone.
Someone, probably my escort with the bland voice
will, in an adjoining room,
push a button.
And that pellet, in the little device
lined up with my ear,
that little packet of deadliness,
will be injected in
with a fierce puff of air.

I am trembling,
tense,
sitting straight up.
I can't help it.

I hear a click.
I jolt –
There was a puff of air.
There is a sense of pressure

Last Night On Earth

this is our last night on earth
tomorrow we leave for the stars –
goodbye mother, goodbye father
goodbye land and time

what shall we do with this last night?
dance with the gravity, sing with the air –
yet we keep stopping
to look up at the stars
their pull is getting stronger

this is our last night, this is our last night on earth
this is the last night of earth
no more nights after this one
no more noon, no more days, no more time
this dream is almost over
we reach our final reality
in the coldness of heaven
tomorrow we leave for the stars

Have You Seen The Sky

have you seen the sky
lately
it seems to have gone missing
I can't remember when I last
saw the blue
and even longer since
the stars at night showed to the naked eye
I thought I saw it
on my way home yesterday
as I walked through the alleys
formed by charcoal high-rises
thought I saw a spot of brightness, a clearing
there was a puffy cloud that would surely
lead to blue
but it was just the steam from an upper vent
I can't remember when I last
saw the sky
have you seen it lately
it's gone missing

Wandering Eye

It's not breaking any vows
but it feels like it is
It's just looking up at the stars
and wishing I were there

What is this yearning
to leave the green behind
what is this dreaming
of ships I can't helm
my eye charts the journey
which always starts from your shores

It's not hurting anyone
well maybe only me
It's just that reaching for the stars
leaves you with aching arms

What is this yearning
to leave the green behind
what is this dreaming
of sleeping under an alien sky
my eye charts the journey
from the home shores of you

It's not breaking any vows
but it feels like it is
It's looking up at the stars
with the Earth at my back

Fallout

where were you when the fallout came, the shitstorm, did you turn off the alarms and go back to sleep, burrow under blankets in denial at what must be a movie reel, did you start digging a bunker so far after the thought, did you buy a bumper sticker to tell the universe it wasn't your fault, elbow your way into the gaping crowds and start chanting

where were you when the fallout came, the indigo afterburn of the enemy ships, the backdraft billowing from thudding doors to flame-licked shelters, the windows shattered so completely into minute flecks, reverted into driven sand, while on the shoreline dunes melted into slick glass

so little time to react, to become reactionary, quickly shown futile, puerile, the cars didn't start, couldn't show off the bumper stickers, the mobs dispersed, there was no one looking down on them from the highrises, the pitchforks and torches and molotov cocktails and bleach bombs dropped from hands that instead went groping after bread, mercy, clean water, and a thousand other things upon which they could not close

where were you when the fallout came, the disaster like special effects, can't CGI that bass strumming of panic in your chest, did you run outside gasping for breath, clumps of hair blown off by the radiation-soaked downwash of the strangers' landing craft

where were you when the fallout came, did you crouch outside, and tilt back your head, mouth open, to catch the shimmering, singeing drifts

PART III

BATTLE

LINES

Earth Earns Her Rings

blast debris by the ton
wreckage of ships long and narrow
with names untranslatable
motives incomprehensible
deadliness incontrovertible

their water supply carried from a planet unnamed
filled approximately 60% of their bulk
flash-frozen and shattered
from miles of ships long and narrow

now we're wedded to Saturn
our huge silent cohabitator
though our rings are narrower
and less refined
but newer and bolder
and earned by calculated destruction
distinct from natural pulverization

though it was a natural reaction
to the ships long and narrow
with common language of violence
we screamed back with all we had
every button pressed, every missile code cracked
blast debris by the ton
ice and dust
we have our rings

Hot Gates

this sword is mine
the weapon is mine
the breath is mine
the air is mine

I am the breath
I am the sword
I am weapon

the sound of stone
the breath of steel
the sense of sword
the dream of life
the thought of now

I move the dream
I drown in sense
in sound and steel
I fall to stone

Desert Legion

onward the soldiers – I watched them go
march off in a dust cloud towards reddening sun
the sand in my eye made me wish I would weep

your hand slips
from my shoulder
bedded limbs
warm against me
I pull cool sheets up over
my legs now straight and long
the song of a bird tells me dawn has arrived
and I can stop telling myself to sleep

in the heat of the day all is yellowed and dry
I make claims of a necessity
then can shape no more words
reaching from the shade you ask me to explain
and in the temple courtyard they are praying for rain

for the dust clouds round the soldiers
and the grit that's in the wine
for the taste of sand on lips
and heat that forces all to cover
for the marchers long dismissed
for no one who would be missed
I stare at the land under the sun

I keep my limbs wrapped from the burning
yet I stare my eyes to parched
I keep my vision on the dryness
I keep my vision of the sand
someone must look upon the rocks
someone must gaze upon the sand
echoes in the emptiness
I make claims of a necessity
that drives me to be still
but even to myself I don't try to explain
and in the temple courtyard they are praying for rain

I make claims of a necessity
outside I listen draped in black
my open eyes roving across the sand
the chanting rises throughout the day
while I proclaim necessity
while you rest in the shade
I don't know why they want the rain
to erode the emptiness
roses never grew here anyway

Figurehead

carve out his ears, his eyes, his affable smile
his glad-hands, his glad rags, his college tie tac
shellac him well so the blood will hose right off
he's the figurehead we need,
get him up there, get him ready
make the best face we can present to the world
don't let him crack, rust, or freeze up

he'll be neater, cleaner, a good listener
picture podium perfect
hide the bolts well
get that expression: "I see the best in you"
present that, represent us
chosen by us masses so we can be left alone
get him up there, shove him out there
we'll just mutter on behind
we'll just putter on below
we'll just let him take the blows
don't let him crack, don't let him rust
carve him now, quickly, perfectly
so we can put him up there
so we can just get on with our lives
and not be on the frontlines
he'll be our headline to the world

We Slaved For Water

we slaved for water
we tugged and hauled and screamed
and ran off into the shadows for respite
dragged back by bonds

we screamed for water
encaved away from sky

we toiled for water
prisoners, bounded, we strained for shore
we ached for that single line

we slaved for water
familiar lashes, old marks
chafed with salt, growing numb
wrapped in blue and green and brown
looking, seeing grey

we died for water
for the privilege of drowning

Homesick

It's too late to lose your soul
you know yourself too well
It's too late to lose your soul
you know yourself too well

Midnight on the streets
and you're up against the wall again
can't keep track of the beat
so you're falling behind again
shouting at the blue coats, cursing all the turn coats
"How can you not do this for your country?"

Midnight on the clock and the riches turn to rags
locked up in the stocks, spit on by the hags
down by one with five to go –
ask them what they think they know
"How can you do this for a lie?"

You soul is with you when you sleep
it's not the Lord's but yours to keep
Waste not want lot
dream not love not
You can throw away your life
but you cannot lose your soul

Midnight over here but it's dawning gold in Ireland
mockeries of fear – what can you do for the homeland
Can't put your trust in man 'cause he doesn't last
gotta put your trust in God 'cause He won't pay cash

It's too late to lose your soul
you can't sell it to the Devil
the Devil doesn't want it
you can't pledge it to the Lord
the good Lord doesn't need it

The Fort and The Old Man

my gun is raised to his forehead
weeping, I ask,
"You are not coming with us?"
it was meant to be a cold demand
emerges rough and anguished
our mentor, our commander
we need our old man, cripple or not
and cripple he is, sitting there with wasted legs
the limbs a mass of recent wounds burned deep

he says calmly, ignoring my gun,
"I am not going to the fort
you will all die there, and you don't need me for that"
"We are going to hold them off!" I manage to snap.
"we must go, or everyone will die here in town."
"I am not going to the fort," he repeats
he does not look ashamed or frightened
or even afraid for us
for us, his troops, his students, his children
what he does look is grey as the stones below his
twisted feet
and he looks as if he has seen this all before

sure, we all have
why is it different this time
perhaps he is ashamed of his weakness
the withered limbs, the thinned voice
but for years we have picked his shouts and his growls
out of the sounds of the fray,
our heartbeats tuned to his steps

eventually, my arm and the gun drop away
he stays on the bench
we go to the fort
without the old man, without our mentor
we go with our pride
and if the old man holds our shame, we leave it behind
yet with flecks of doubt over an old, beaten,
          burned man

we go to the fort
and we die
we all die
I do not learn what happens to the old man

Welcome

Dark fortress walls
loom high, matching mountains and the pines
You welcome me
as you leave

One by one, the stars fall
dopplering hisses onto the field
melting into the courtyard
Stones of rough ebon and smooth shadow
soak up the sparks

For you I slew the phoenix
ripped the clouds
burnt my palms on the lightning
quenched the blazing feathers

For you I made my way here
Dark fortress walls
loom high
You welcome me
as you leave

PART IV

SONGS

<u>Lord of Misrule</u>

for Johnny the Rhymer

The Lord of Misrule
pays his taxes, quietly
plays his mandolin nightly
his throne room is narrow
and as deep as his growl
loyal retainers
follow him on the prowl
wend through the streets
each evening's parade
the world upside down
is turned every day

Turn My Wine Back Into Water

She's the sliver under my skin
the sunset that comes again and again
She's the vampire that drains me dry
She sees my soul with gold-lashed eyes
Sirocco winds for her blow hotter
turn my wine back into water

I took a walk on the desert's edge
saw a serpent sunning on the ledge
Some god jumped out from behind a tree
said he was gonna have to punish me
Strange enough, he's never caught her
she's her own, not just Eve's daughter

Welcome mirage of a dirty city
thought I'd never seen something so pretty
Come on, babe, show me around
I've never been in this part of town
She pulled me in and my rope grew tauter
oh, turn my wine back into water

I came up to a curtained stall
and wanted to buy a drink
but all the fellow gave me
was a cracker and a wink
I didn't share no secret with him
but I was beginning to understand
I could keep on picking up sand
but it would run right out of my hand
Just when I thought I'd never see
a cool young thing again
she appeared and offered me
a juicy apple red as sin
I looked for the merchant
    now that I'd something to barter
but the mage disappeared, a trick he'd taught her

I carried that apple in a pocket
until it began to rot
I gave up and with the shifting sands
I threw in my poor lot
When all hope had been burned away
by the lonelies and the sun
she was there and asking me
what did I think I'd done
I said she was no more than what I'd thought her
and would she turn my wine back into water

She's the wound that just won't heal
she's the player who will not deal
Time after eon I thought she was gone
then I'd glimpse her in blue and she'd lead me on
through a million summers I must've sought her
a million naked looks I must've shot her

I asked her if this world was real
she asked me, What do you think
I said, Well all I want is you
and maybe a little drink
She laughed until she hit the ground
sprites carried her off in a litter
leaving me with sunburned arms
and a mouth that was awfully bitter
and I swear if and when I could've bought her
I'd make her turn my wine back into water

Western

He was a mystery man
with a doom set on his head
he rode into town
and he painted it red
he pulled all the sinners right out of their beds
he rode into town and he painted it red

Welcome to Hell
what have you got to lose
handful of cards and some rotgut booze
he was their mystery man
with a brand around his neck
he rode into town
and called it Devil's Wreck

Welcome to Hell
what have you got to gain
redemption in bullets and a hint at his name
he was their mystery man
with a ghost around his head
he rode into town
and he painted it red

Ziggy

there you go
soaring off to the stars again
there you go
drifting between suns again

you keep me waiting up for you
lying on the grass
staring up at the night
you keep me holding my breath for you
thinking of you high
weightless in the vacuum

Oh Ziggy won't you come down
Oh Ziggy won't you come home

that darkness between the stars
empty spaces cold
spaces none can fill
that darkness between the stars
I'm left looking cold
weightless without your mass

there you go
soaring off to the stars again
there you go
drifting between suns again

Oh Ziggy won't you come down
Oh Ziggy won't you come home

January Magician

please just sit down and I'll get you a drink
we can talk about what you think you saw
there's ice on the sidewalks
it's ten hours til sunrise
this is not the time to go

please don't get up, Jack and Cokes all around
I can tell you what you didn't quite see
there's tricks in just glimpses
no one left out the back door
this is not the time to go

please take off your coat and unwind your scarf
we can talk about what you think you saw
there's ice in your vision
let me warm up your hands
this is not the time to go

please don't go out, don't leave in January
I can tell you what you really saw
mirrors for my stage act
no one's here but us two
this is not the time to go

please don't walk out, you haven't finished your drink
don't you want to hear about my latest trick
there's ice on the sidewalks
it's ten hours til sunrise
this is not the time to go

Where Did Your Eyes Go

where did your eyes go
while I sent her away
why didn't you see
what she did to me
do you think me unjust
do you do what you must
where did your eyes go
when she did this to us

this kind of ambience doesn't come cheap
one small misstep and you fall in the deep
whirling ocean below
you almost know
how to scale the steep cliff
how to bridge the gold rift
but my words slip away
you did not hear me say
that she left today

this casual ambience didn't come cheap
when she left we slipped back into the cold deep
whirling ocean below
I know you know
not to scale the steep cliff
not to bridge the gold rift
why didn't you see
what she did to me
your sight did not stray
when she was told to stay
where did your eyes go
when I sent her away

Old Tricks

I won't let you
get up to your old tricks again

I have seen you disappear
I have seen this trick before
I know about the pulleys
I know about the three trap doors
I won't let you slip away again
I have seen your tricks before

You can do it on the stage
for a naïve audience
You can fade away before their eyes
the supreme man of confidence
You won't pull it off at home though
I've learned warning signs of transience
And I have watched closely while
you performed this trick before

You may do it for the thrill
do it for the pure prestige
significance in your gestures
nothing up your sleeves
but I won't let you
get up to your old tricks again

Grace With Gravity – Plainsong

everything has fallen
everything has fallen
everything has fallen into place
everything has fallen into grace
with gravity

I'll brush your fingers one more time
brushstroke paint to canvas
finishing your lines
polishing your nails
blushing your cheeks
sharpening the nails
on which everything has fallen

on which everything has fallen into place
like butterflies impaled
sunk into windowed cases
just in case they fall
in case they fall too far
for recollection

I brush your fingers one more time
and feel that I have fallen
I feel that I have fallen into place
I feel that I have fallen
with infinite grace
along the lines of gravity
the painted strokes of everything
everything has fallen into place
everything has fallen into infinite grace
with gravity

PART V

NOISE

Reason To Sleep Late

I get up, I read the paper
I don't do the dishes
I blink into the morning
stumble to my feet
reach for the pen
getting the midnight disease
in the unflattering dawn

that swirl of elation
the post-coital comedown
its taint on everything
that runs through your head
writing a poem in the morning
fucks up your entire day

Book Cut

I bled all over Philip K. Dick
the book I checked out from the library
six months, in there at least once a week
and never seen a Philip K. Dick book
in there before this
not even 'Do Androids Dream of Electric Sheep'
yes, the Blade Runner one
but here is, yellowed and now blooded,
'I Hope I Shall Arrive Soon'
Read it before, the title story
not the others though, not all
A tear in my hand, bleeding like a paper cut
I'm sure it's Philip K. Dick's fault
an hour later I'm still bleeding
He would probably say
I'm just stuck over and over
at the minute of cutting
but finishing the book hasn't got me out of this
it just made a bigger mess

My Surgery

full of proper nouns
and trademarks
Foley catheter
Pfannenstiel skin incision
Metzenbaum scissors
O'Connor-O'Sullivan retractor
Heaney suture
Jorgenson scissors
Kocher clamps
Vicryl stitches
3M Telfa dressing
after all the patents and labels
my name on my body

Wanted

when I find the mad bugger whose wall this is
there's going to be a very cathartic mess

Mirror Mirror

mirror mirror on the wall
mirror shatter glass and fall
mirror mirror won't you let me see
reflect something different back to me

the fruit trees growing so crooked
the young girls growing so tall
the wild birds fighting over plums
the young gods trying to keep up

I can't keep up
keep on moving through the mist
early morning fog that never burns away
sloshing in dew up to my ankles
eating apples til I'm sick

so what is this world
and why am I alive in it
so what is this world
and who am I to trust in it
where have all the soldiers gone

mirror mirror on the lake
mirror gives back what it takes
mirror mirror won't you let me dive
back out through to the other side

the tall girls growing so pretty
the dark plums ripen so young
the young birds fighting for seasons
the wild gods scrambling to keep up

I can't keep up
keep on drowning in the dew
early morning light that never turns to noon
romanticizing in the mists
I won't take much more of this

so where is this world
and how do I get out of it
so where is the line
and how do I fight to it
where have all the soldiers gone
so where is the door
and how do I push through to it
so what is this mist
and how do I burn through it
where have all the flamethrowers gone

We Need The Eyes

- grandma thinks she's a Lovecraftian horror
from the madness beyond the void.
- that's awful, why don't you take her to the doctor?
- well, we would, but we need the eyes.

Paris

I kissed her hand and
her fingers were frozen wine
the empire was burning while
somewhere a piper played

The clasp shuddered and fell apart
burnished rose-fire gold
my cloak slipped from my shoulders
crumbling into ash

A tiger's-eye winked at me from her throat
the Laws are crumbling with the city walls
sickness like a rotting peach
the Litany is lost
Helen is seized
the dove will not return with signs of land

In the throne room
her fingernails were bits of rainbow
The wild horse struck at the marble floor
sending up sparks like the queen's gold-flecked eyes
fools and courtiers scrambled to safety
The Harper of Avalon did not move
the blazing, frothing horse
reared past him with rolling mad eyes

Her brow of a romantic's ivory
Her bosom of a lost child's pillow
Her hair of a magician's silk
Her eyes of Ashteroth's stars

Brocade

Come to me, my flower
There is no God to condemn us
there is no Goddess to condone us
Arise, my flower, and talk to me no more
I have heard all your stories already

Sometimes
we smile
Sometimes
I lie on the tiles
wishing and whispering
wanting the moon in my hands

Greet me with your cheerful lies
Douse the fire in your petals

Will you open in the sunlight?
Will you drink up the rain,
the ache of the earth, and my sighs?
Will you shudder and wilt
in the vase on my table?

Mirrored in the clouds
approaching reflection
heeding misdirection
healing contemplation

Sometimes the tiles are cold
I wash my hands again and again
You compromise yourself for me
Sometimes the tiles are cold

Tonight the tiles are cold
Tonight the ruins are old
Tonight my soul is sold
You did not come in time
There is no sound from the sky

PART VI

SIGNALS

<u>Feedback</u>

there's too much noise
and not enough signal
wait, you're breaking up
wait

I'll echo your mangled message
will you listen to yourself
I'll echo your mangled message
see if you can change it
into a clear cascade

there's noise in all your lines
a static which relays to me a message
can you listen to yourself
our voices never sound the same in our own ears
can you make out what you're saying
through the feedback of your ego
and the static of your habits
can you hear the background signal
wait, you're breaking up
wait

The Dead Like To Talk

a common line
the dead like to talk
a vampire finds himself surrounded by ghosts
the medium has to sort through all the chatter
"No, not you, anyone else named Nigel here?
Look, shut up about the cat, if it's not with you
it's been fed. Now I need Nigel Harrington.
Now, please."
All these voices on the wind
no sleep for the psychic
there's life after death and it's filled
with gossip
and with idle speculation
about what will happen to the living
"My Sharon will get into NYU, you just
wait and see."
"Oh yeah? My grandson's going to Harvard."
"He's two years old."
"Wait and see."
What's happening
where did all these currents come from
ask them, ask the living, they understand
why are they always asking us for answers?

common as dirt, the dead
their voices outnumber the living
outdrown the messages from further beyond
were there any
The lich followed by spectres
The explorer opening the tomb, puff of stale air
and whirlwind of spirits
all wanting to ask
what year is it
who is king
where did you get those shoes

They tell you about fish they saw
as they drifted along the seabed
from the shipwreck to the shore
They talk about each other
speculate on hauntings and hoaxes
Possess terrified young nuns
just to talk dirty
they miss sex so much

The dead are a chatty bunch
a common thread
in books, in movies, in games
whispering, instructing,
we listen
through the babble hoping for a back of beyond
through the noise for a signal
we listen
and listen for the uncommon line

Alpha Male

you were the first, she shrugs
you won't be the last
the alpha but not the omega too

alpha male
king for a day
six months at the outside

you were the first, she shrugs
don't tell me I'll be your last
don't pretend that brooding
over this brief romance
will fill up your date book

I gave you all the thanks I owed
called out your name with pleasure
I won't pretend I didn't
you know, before I met you
I had heard of sex
don't act so shocked that I'll move on
after all
you moved on once too
that bed would never have held us
twined together otherwise

you were the first, she shrugs
you won't be the last
so roll on out and
answer me this
how much longer do you think
you can be an alpha male
when your conquests all end up
looking for an omega

When You Said

lost in this whitewashed maze
led by your metallic eyes
fed with your industrial lies
I should have listened when you said goodbye

you locked the doors with deadbolts
you shut out the living me
I break into what was my home
I should have listened when you said goodbye

curling ferns on the window sill
a battery pack and an electric bill
home could have been more than this
you should have returned my kiss

half-smoked cigarette in the ashtray
a few clean dishes all put away
you should have returned my kiss
home could have been more than this

firm of color, void of hue
your filed steel fingers on my lips
over your flat eyes I trip
I should have listened when you said goodbye

Space between the throne and the wall

space between the throne and the wall
cramped: a gnome for her play
She puts her back to me
there are no windows, only
shy yellow candles
I want to leave, or just
to move
Far enough – her vulnerable spine
her unguarded kidneys
her warm flesh and cold blood
Freedom –
I know, see this much
She holds the keys
she holds my passport
my eyes are tired of this room
these light-mares, candles,
of breathing smoke
Her blue-blood feet rooted to the marble floor
Her burning hair braided into the tapestries
Her coat of arms clutching
if anyone could, I would leave
If my eyes weren't busy watering from
the candles' smoke,
I would cry.
If my heart weren't beating in her bloodied hands,
I would feel.
To dive off the barren cliff,
run out the barricaded double doors
cut the velvet ties
– I cannot, for
this is the same country
and the wench still lives.

Seventh Circle

full of dampness, rot, dew and salt and garden
perfumes, you move before the windows, a silhouette
against the twilight which I swear has come so early,
so precipitously

your ribbons slice the stars

longer than your hair trail the slippery, shining
streams, pinned at your blonde scalp

the view from lying flat on the bed: windows so tall as
to seem to curve inward at the top, gleam of burnished
curtain rods, cascades of fabric cream shot with
copper, perfectly supple enough for waves in the
breeze, strong tidal pulls of fabric, the design catching
residual light to show fiery sparks – lift my head, crane
my neck, strain my vision, glimpse of woad-blue
counterpane piled up at my bare feet, toes chill

I didn't know the seventh circle had three towering
windows and joined onto a half-wild garden

flashing silver scissors in the starlight, their
movements of cold fire visible through the windows,
glass panes pushed open, I watch in silence while you
dance a slow waltz through the garden, dipping
movements with your sharp device, half-hidden by a
thick-tendriled bush, then emerging with a swan's
curve to reach for a vine twisted around an arbor, the
paint long gone from the woven wood, ivy more sturdy
than the cracking slats

you cut blush roses and aurum lilies and trailings of
bridal wreath with the deadly shears – bring in armful
after armful, saturate this room with flowers, dripping
in bulbous stoneware vases on the floor, and empty
liquor bottles on shelves and dressers – small and
narrow cordials tinted fir green, square blue glass of
Bombay gin, weak emerald of wines, river mud of
Trappist beers, the clear to match vodka ones turned
murky with handfuls of stems, thorns, and untrimmed
leaves

Hell is murky, to be sure

but I didn't know the seventh circle had an old-
fashioned poster bed, four cherry wood poles carved
spiraling up to the sky – no canopy – no one told me
about the windows, walls, doors – no roof – only clear
midnight sky above – I couldn't predict that it would be
brimming with flowers

your sandals discarded by the door, covered in wet
grass and mud and flecks of flimsy white petals,
sandals of delicate strips impossible to prevent your
feet getting the same treatment, dirt in your toes, petals
clinging wetly to ankles, smudging the thin striped rug,
the pale cotton sheets as you kneel on the bed

your head bends and your ribbons slice the stars

an unnamable color these rippling lengths, some
shadowed petal bruised mouth hue

in this gloaming, a cup of water touched to my lips,
cool, slightly mineral, I imagine I taste also the sienna
clay of the vessel

the dark becomes more perfect, the alien constellations
brighter, I sigh with resignation, with contentment,
with damned comfort

you lean over me and your ribbons slice the stars

Dare
for J.B.

you dared
me to eat a
peach. or possibly to
kiss your mouth and smudge my lip gloss
I did.
it was
just as I feared
moist, sweet, much longer than
strictly necessary, and made
me late.

Pearl

tell me of the bird in your hood
golden eyes peering out from the fur lining
why is it here with you on this plane
leaving Barrow in the lime-streaked Arctic evening
why, in the seat in front of mine
is there a small speckled bird nestled in the hood
of a girl with a face like a pearl

Cypher

A to B
glyph to C
blood to stone
stone to rune
rune to letter
I got your message
I'm cracking the cypher
kiss to coin
coin to note
I'm getting the message
I have the message nearly decoded

your communiqués found encrypted
clues left near every door
wand at the bedroom
disc in the kitchen
a sequence of numbers
written in cobalt by the front lock
symbols left by my alchemist lover
silver to glass
heat to hands
cold to mouth
another rotor turned

in your enigma machine
the many wheels of your heart
I read your cypher
A to B
dove to angel
angel to sword
sword to field
field to road

the code breaking down
the message came through clear
road to note
blood to stone
substitution
I got your message
loud and clear

Author's Note

Thanks to my brother Patrick, my parents, my unofficial brother Brian Komarny, Edie Nally, Johnny the Rhymer, and everyone else who kept asking me if it was done yet.

More thanks than I can express to Ted Kern, for listening to my ideas for the cover image, and making it come to life in a truly gorgeous way. Ted, you are a star.

Big cheers to Scott Lanes, for spending quality time on my little shoots.

Thank you to Alex Panos, for promoting my first book, *Light Shift*, and being an all-around great guy to know.

Hugs and smooches to Melissa Penta, for being a crazy friend and doing my crazy hair.

And thank you to my husband, Joel Bryant, for love, humor, strength, and invaluable help assembling bookcases, bitching about software, and wrangling cats.

ABOUT THE AUTHOR

Annie Boyle lives in Salem, Massachusetts
with her husband and two cats.
She has been published in various print and
online magazines. *Age of Miracles* is her
second published collection of poetry.
Her first book, *Light Shift*, is also available
through lulu.com.

Please visit the author's website at
www.lulu.com/annie_boyle
for more information on and directions for
ordering signed/inscribed copies of her work.

Ms. Boyle may be emailed at
ak_boyle@yahoo.com
for requests and feedback.
Please include the relevant book title(s) or
"Annie Boyle poetry" in the subject line.